THE LETTERS
OF VINCENT VAN GOGH

MARK ROSKILL was the holder of scholarships to Eton and to Trinity College, Cambridge, where he graduated in Classics with first class honours. He then turned to the study of art history and has had teaching posts in the United States: at Princeton and now at the Fogg Art Museum, Harvard. He is the author of a book on English Painting and *Van Gogh, Gauguin and the Impressionist Circle* (1970).

THE LETTERS OF VINCENT VAN GOGH

Selected, Edited and Introduced by
MARK ROSKILL

A TOUCHSTONE BOOK
Published by Simon & Schuster

NEW YORK

TOUCHSTONE
Rockefeller Center
1230 Avenue of the Americas
New York, NY 10020

First Touchstone Edition 1997

Manufactured in the United States of America

3 5 7 9 10 8 6 4

Library of Congress Catalog Card Number: 63-13089

ISBN: 0-684-84300-5

EDITORIAL NOTE

The English text of the *Letters* presented here is basically taken from the three-volume edition published by Constable in 1927/29; and thanks are due to the proprietors of that edition and to the Engineer V. W. van Gogh for their co-operation in permitting its re-use. Thirty years after the first and only appearance of that edition, it has seemed appropriate to use my editorial licence rather freely in the making of textual revisions of various kinds, and the recording of omissions that have since come to light. Similarly I have included in the form of additional footnotes a certain amount of explanatory comment on persons, places or situations that are referred to, together with translations of such quotations or special phrases as are given in French within the letters themselves, and a few incidental observations of a broader sort that may interest the general reader.

Each letter selected for inclusion has been captioned with its place of origin and a date. Letters that were dated by van Gogh himself are given with their original headings; for the most part, however, the artist refrained from dating his letters, and in all such cases a conjectural date in square brackets has been given. The sources for these conjectural dates are threefold. Some of them go back to the earliest editorial work carried out by Mme. J. van Gogh-Bonger—and in certain cases are based on evidence or reasoning that can no longer be reconstructed. Others are owed to a series of articles recently published in the Dutch periodical *Maatstaf* by Dr. Jan Hulsker of The Hague; I am personally grateful to Dr. Hulsker for his permission to make use of his findings for the present edition, and though I have kept to a rather broader system of date-brackets than the one he presented himself, I would like to make warm acknowledgement of the assistance received from this quarter. The third and final source has been my own research, independent from that of

Dr. Hulsker; study of the Arles letters in another connection had equipped me with a scheme of dates in this area which indeed largely agrees with his, and I have also, for this edition specifically, re-checked some of Dr. Hulsker's findings and worked over the periods not covered in his articles.

The choice of plates has been made with a view to providing a conspectus of van Gogh's artistic development, and also with a view to illustrating some of the principal subjects or treatments that are referred to in the letters selected.

My thanks are due to Mr. Richard Ollard of Collins for watching over the destiny of this book from first to last, and to my wife for all kinds of help that made progress speedier and more pleasant.

M. R.

NOTE : Apart from a few minor changes of punctuation the Memoir of Vincent by his sister-in-law has been reprinted here exactly as it first appeared.

CONTENTS

PLATES
(*between page* 160 *and* 161)

INTRODUCTION

There are two great works of the nineteenth century which, more than any other writings of the time, give us a sense of what it was like to be a real creator in the visual arts during that marvellously rich and strenuous era. The inner order which they possess is not based on any literary kind of design, but stems from the character and momentum of the painter's life itself. One of them is the Journal of Eugène Delacroix; the other is the correspondence of Vincent van Gogh.

If we want an analogy nearer our own day to van Gogh's total personality—its strength of character, powers of insight, and rough-hewn forcefulness of language—we may find it in the correspondence of D. H. Lawrence. The ways in which the two men suffered and their ideals for art and society were in many ways akin. Despite the laborious and searing character of the struggles of both men to survive materially, to love sincerely and to create, one can equally say of the letters of van Gogh what was written very recently about those of Lawrence: "no-one halfway alive could be untouched by the joy of living that breathes in the slightest of them."[1]

What sort of value and importance do the *Letters to Theo* have for today's reader? The answer is fourfold. First of all they provide a narrative of van Gogh's life. They unfold its main events and disclose in so doing a wealth of passing thoughts and small factual details:

Now I have met Christine [i.e. Sien]. As you know, she was pregnant, ill, out in the cold; I was all by myself ... I took to her, though not immediately with the idea

[1] "Friends and Enemies," *Times Literary Supplement,* 27 April 1962.

of marrying her; but when I got to know her better, it became plain to me that if I wanted to help her, I had to do it seriously . . . she said, " I will stay with you, however poor you may be." And this is how it all came about.

(May, 1882)

Today I saw Dr. Gachet again and I am going to paint at his house on Tuesday morning, then I shall dine with him and afterwards he will come to look at my paintings. He seems very sensible, but he is as discouraged about his job as a country doctor as I am about my painting. Then I said to him that I would gladly exchange job for job.

(May, 1890)

Always informative and often most moving from such a point of view, they speak on this count for themselves (with the memoir by the artist's sister-in-law, reprinted here, to fill in the early background and supply necessary strands of continuity). At the same time, too, we learn from them the influences to which van Gogh was subject at differing times—what books he read and how he reacted to them, in what ways the works of other artists appealed to him (especially the older masters whom he had cause to admire), what thinkers nourished his own philosophy of art :

I remember quite well having been very much impressed . . . by a drawing by Daumier, an old man under the chestnut trees in the Champs Elysées (an illustration for Balzac) . . . [there was] something so strong and manly in Daumier's conception that I thought, it must be a good thing to think and feel that way, and to overlook or pass by many things in order to concentrate on things that provide food for thought, and touch us as human beings more directly and personally than meadows or clouds. And so I always feel greatly drawn to the figures either of the English graphic artists or of the

English authors, because of their Monday-morning-like sobriety and studied simplicity and gravity and analytical candour, as something solid and robust which can give us strength in our times of weakness. The same holds good, among French authors, for Balzac and Zola too.   (October, 1882)

I have been re-reading Dickens' *Christmas Books* these days. There are things in them so profound that one must read them over and over; there are tremendously close connections with Carlyle.   (April, 1889)

Comments like these tell us not only the kind of man that van Gogh was, but also the way in which his essential ideas grew up and took wing.

Secondly, the letters document the succession of paintings and drawings in a very rich way. Indispensable in this way to the scholar (who uses them in detail for the construction of a full chronology), they have also the more general interest of giving, in many instances, a running commentary upon work in progress :

This week I have done some rather large studies in the woods, and I tried to put into these more vigour and finish than the first ones had. The one which I believe succeeded best is of nothing but a piece of dug-up earth —white, black and brown sand after a downpour of rain. Here and there the clods of earth caught the light and stood out in bold relief. After I had been sitting sketching that patch of ground for quite a while, there was another violent thunderstorm with a tremendous cloudburst, which went on for at least an hour. I was so keen to resume work that I stayed at my post and sheltered myself as well as I could behind a large tree.

(August, 1882)

I have a model at last—a Zouave—a lad with a small face, the neck of a bull, the eye of a tiger, and I began with one portrait and made a fresh start with another; the half-length that I did of him was fearfully harsh, in a uniform the colour of saucepans enamelled with blue, with braids of a faded russet-orange, and two stars on his breast, an ordinary blue and really hard to do. His feline and highly bronzed head, with its reddish cap, I focused against a green door and the orange bricks of a wall.   (June, 1888)

Passages like these portray, for one particular canvas or another, the context of the creative process.

Then again the letters are a source of psychological insight. First and foremost they show us the inner workings of van Gogh's relationship with his brother; for example:

I am writing specially in order to tell you how thankful I am for your visit. It was a long time since we had seen each other or corresponded, as we used to do. It is better, all told, to be friends than to be dead to one another . . . The hours that we spent together have at least given us the assurance that we are both still in the land of the living. When I saw you again and walked with you, I had a feeling of the kind which I used once to experience more than I do now—a feeling that life was, so to say, something good and precious which one ought to value; and I felt more cheerful and alive than I had for a long time.   (October, 1879)

And then, over and above this, they illumine such things as the artist's rate of work,

I am always afraid of not working enough; I think I can do so much better still, and that is what I am aiming for, sometimes with a kind of fury.   (May, 1883)

I shall be all in when the " Orchards " are over . . . We would not have too many of them, even if I could bring

off twice as many ... You will see that the rose-coloured
peach trees were painted with a certain passion. I must
also have a starry night with cypresses, or perhaps sur-
mounting a field of ripe corn ... I am in a continual
fever of work. (April, 1888)

the ever nervous and broken quality of his pictorial hand
writing,

Here is a sketch of an orchard ... It's absolutely clear
and absolutely straight off the cuff. A frenzy of impastos
faintly tinged with yellow and lilac, worked into a body
of paint that was initially white. (April, 1888)

... Nowadays I am putting pressure on myself to find
a brushwork without stippling or anything else, nothing
but the varied stroke. (August, 1888)

The "Olives" ... are exaggerations from the point of
view of arrangement, their lines are warped like the
ones you find in old forests. (September, 1889)

and the underlying tenor of his imagery:

I have two new drawings now, one of a man reading his
Bible and the other of a man saying grace before his
dinner, which is out on the table ... My intention in
these two ... is one and the same; namely to express the
peculiar sentiment of Christmas and the New Year. In
Holland and England alike this is always more or less
religious ... (December, 1882)

Spring is tender, green young corn and pink apple
blossoms. Autumn is the contrast of the yellow leaves
against violet tones. Winter is the snow with black
silhouettes. (June/July 1884)

Passages such as these make plain how well van Gogh was capable of knowing his desires, and with what control he could set out to realize them.

Lastly one can draw out of the letters revealing parallels to van Gogh's total output of paintings, its constants and its variables. Descriptions of sights in nature that amount to "unpainted pictures" can be compared year by year in their imagery with actual contemporaneous treatments of landscape or figure subjects:

Yesterday . . . in the Noordeinde [part of The Hague] I saw workmen busy pulling down the section opposite the palace, fellows all white with lime dust, with drays and horses. It was cool, windy weather, the sky was grey and the spot was very characteristic.

Then two other larger compositions of labourers in the dunes . . . are the things I should most like to finish. Long rows of diggers—paupers employed by the muni-cipality—before a patch of sandy ground, which has to be dug.

(July, 1883)

This morning I saw the country from my window a long time before sunrise, with nothing but the morning star, which looked very big.

I have two landscapes in hand . . . views taken into the hills, one is the country that I see from the window of my bedroom. In the foreground a field of corn ruined and cast to the ground after a storm. A boundary wall, and beyond the grey foliage of a few olive-trees, some huts and the hills. Finally at the top of the canvas a great white and grey cloud drowned in the azure.

(June, 1889)

Similarly van Gogh's ways of translating the ideas and theories of others into personal terms can be compared with the "translations" that he did in line or paint after the works of earlier masters—Rembrandt, Millet, Delacroix:

Meanwhile, I have started on copying the Millets. The "Sower" is finished, and I have sketched the "Four Hours of the Day."

I told him plainly: "De Bock, . . . if we do not draw the figure or draw trees as if they were figures, we are people without backbone, or else with a weak one. Do you think Millet and Corot, whom we both love so much, could draw figures, yes or no? I think those masters could do anything.

(May and October, 1881)

Alone or almost alone amongst painters Rembrandt has . . . that heartbroken tenderness, that glimpse into a superhuman infinitude that seems so natural there; you come upon it in many places in Shakespeare.

I am perhaps going to try to work from Rembrandt. I have especially an idea of doing the "Man at Prayer" in the colour-scale that runs from light yellow up to violet.

(June/July, 1889 and May, 1890)

Another most suggestive analogy between the letters and the paintings involves the interplay of past and present. One can look for correspondences in the comparative importance of their roles at different times, and in the ways in which they were brought into synthesis with one another. For example:

I think that the town of Arles was infinitely more glorious once as regards the beauty of its women and the beauty of its costumes. Now everything has a worn and sickly look about it. But when you look at it for long, the old charm revives.

Do you remember that wonderful page in *Tartarin* [i.e. *Tartarin de Tarascon* by Alphonse Daudet], the complaint of the old Tarascon stage-coach? Well, I have just painted that red and green vehicle in the courtyard of the inn . . . Here's to the country of good old Tartarin, I am enjoying myself in it more and more, and it is going to become our second fatherland.

(September and October, 1888)

I shall attack the cypresses and the mountains. I think that this will be the core of the work that I have done here and there in Provence . . .

I am thinking of doing a new version of the picture of peasants at dinner with the lamplight effect [i.e. the *Potato-Eaters* of 1885] . . . Then, if you like, I will do the old tower of Nuenen again and the cottage.

(November, 1889 and April, 1890)

In particular the question of how much his Dutch background continued to mean to van Gogh during his later years in France can fruitfully be studied by looking at the two sorts of record side by side :

Involuntarily—is it the effect of this Ruysdael country? [Jacob Ruysdael was a Dutch landscapist of the seventeenth century]—I keep thinking of Holland, and across the twofold remoteness of distance and of time gone by these memories have a kind of heartbreak in them.

What I learnt in Paris [sc. about painting] *is leaving me*, and . . . I am returning to the ideas I had in the country before I knew the impressionists.

(July and August, 1888)

And the answer that comes back from such extracts and others like them is undoubtedly in favour of Holland.

All in all, the *Letters to Theo* are a supremely eloquent record of the ways in which van Gogh's art and life interacted with one another. One particularly telling and wideranging example of such interaction is the history told there of van Gogh's appreciation of Japanese art, and its influence on his attitude to the South of France during and after his move to Provence in the spring of 1888. One of van Gogh's reasons for going South came from his discovery of Japanese prints in Antwerp at the end of 1885.[1] During the subsequent two years spent in Paris this original, limited interest widened considerably. In Paris he saw the formal influence of Japanese art extending right across the generation of " impressionist" painters—to use his own blanket term—to which he then attached himself. Out of this, van Gogh developed an inescapable sense of commitment. He saw it as desirable that the " return to nature" of the impressionists be extended still further, and the South, with its natural colouring and bright sunshine, offered a "second Japan." Faced also with his own unhappiness and ill-health, he looked to a climate in which his own modes of feeling would assimilate themselves to those of Japanese painters. He felt it important to investigate what Japanese art would convey, when studied against and within the landscape of this " second Japan"; he was to hang Japanese prints on the walls of his studio just as soon as he took over the Yellow House at Arles, and from the very first he was to see the local countryside (under snow as well as in sunshine) as mirroring the major motifs of Japanese nature-painting. He believed that other artists beside himself could acquire an awareness of how the drawing and colour in Japanese prints were vehicles for the Oriental artists' feelings towards nature. Individuality of expression and technical expansion would then freely bene-

[1] He had known something of Japanese art as far back as his days in Nuenen, but the revelation of Japanese line and colour together came only now.

fit; and European nature-painting as a whole, present and future, would thereby gain immeasurably:

. . . Other artists will rise up in this lovely country [i.e. Provence] and do for it what the Japanese have done for theirs.

(May, 1888)

Most concrete of all was van Gogh's idea of establishing a colony in the South; a community, that is, to which a whole group of Parisian artists could periodically move—following the path that he had taken himself for the time being—whenever too much exposure to the dank climate of the metropolis and its moral and social hurly-burly put them in need of a change of scene and a refreshment of the sensibility. More than that, once the group arrangement was established, the "studio of the South" would offer an atmosphere that was sunny in its co-operative spirit as well as being warmed by natural sunshine. Under such conditions, the straight-forward, simple values exemplified in Japanese art could be nourished, in place of the spiritually damaging effects of social convention and intellectual over-education; for the "clearer sky" of the South seems to have symbolized for van Gogh a moral order founded upon clarity and simplicity. Besides the practical consequences of companionship and cheaper living, van Gogh envisioned also a further co-operative venture (itself modelled on Japanese precedent) for the exchange of works between artists in different centres. In sum, as the scheme of ideas crystallized that committed van Gogh to his great campaign of work in the South of France, four different sorts of concern drove it along: æsthetic, practical, metaphysical and humane. And the letters show how each and all of these concerns were bound up in van Gogh's urge to live his life to the full.

It was in 1893, only three years after Vincent's suicide, that the first batch of his letters to his brother Theo to appear in print came out in the *Mercure de France*. Emile Bernard,

Vincent's friend and correspondent who had already arranged memorial exhibitions of his work, was responsible for their publication. More letters were subsequently printed in the same magazine, and Theo's widow, Mme. J. van Gogh-Bonger, took on the task of transcribing and editing the whole sequence of letters that, over eighteen years, Theo had so faithfully preserved. The first collected edition was published in 1914, and further letters have come to light since then. In all, some 670 of the letters that Vincent wrote to Theo are known to-day to have survived.

The present edition is the only one to offer a small and representative group of letters, each of which has some special distinction of its own. It is also the only one to give the reader the maximum of editorial help, as he moves along from subject to subject or from one letter to another.

While the earliest of the extant letters dates from 1872, it was not until mid-1880 that the correspondence opened up and acquired a powerful inner rhythm of its own, which only van Gogh's death would interrupt. Before that time, while Vincent was in turn representative for a firm of art-dealers, schoolmaster, bookshop assistant, student preparing for the University and lay preacher, he had written to Theo as the occasion prompted; and the subject of art was mentioned only incidentally, in reference to a picture or print or spectacle of nature that had appealed to him, or in regard to a sketch that he had done. The first letter that dealt explicitly and at length with Vincent's desire and ambition to become an artist was written in July 1880—it appears in this selection:

> But you will ask: What is your definite aim? That aim becomes more definite, will stand out slowly and surely, just as the rough draft becomes a sketch, and the sketch becomes a picture . . .

From then on, for almost exactly ten years, Theo loyally continued to provide the financial support which had originally enabled his brother to commit himself completely to painting. He did this in the form of regular payments out of his own salary as a dealer. And throughout the decade in question Vincent wrote to Theo with an equal regularity; though it is exceptional for his letters of this period to carry precise dates, it would seem that in normal circumstances the artist must have written at least once a week, and sometimes twice weekly or even twice in a single day (excluding that two-year period between 1886 and 1888 when the brothers were sharing rooms in Paris). Concurrently, there were certain other familiars with whom Vincent communicated regularly—extended sequences of letters survive that went to his sister Wil and to his artist friends Anthon van Rappard and Emile Bernard. But in none of these cases was the correspondence anywhere nearly as heavy as that with Theo; and almost invariably, where the subject matter treated is identical, it is the account to Theo that was more detailed and explicit.

What began, then, as an exchange of personal news between highly affectionate brothers temporarily separated developed into a phenomenon of far broader scope. It is not simply the fact of sheer quantity. Owing in part to the power of attraction exerted in our time by the artistic personality as such—a power of attraction extending to every available private and intimate detail of an artist's thought and conduct—there is a strong tendency to regard Vincent's letters to Theo as simply a "confessional" record, a convenient means for Vincent to unload his immediate feelings. If indeed the artist is to be looked on as a romantic figure, standing apart from the everyday world and unfettered by its conventions, then van Gogh, it may be held, poignantly epitomizes such a condition. But to accept the above interpretation solely and entirely is to disregard the strong element of calculation in van Gogh's personality, a very complex element even more conspicuous in the correspondence with Theo than in the paintings themselves.

The major clue here is the direct relationship between what Vincent wrote and what Theo was paying him. It is scarcely a coincidence that the increase of correspondence after mid-1880 followed upon Theo's pledge of financial support; that its mood and tempo fluctuated on Vincent's side according as he felt that Theo's attitude gave cause for alarm; or that the first of Vincent's mental breakdowns was closely associated with the news of Theo's imminent marriage and the clear threat this imposed on Theo's capacity to go on providing for him. Enough, moreover, survives of Theo's side of the correspondence—some forty letters, all dating from the last four years of Vincent's life—to make plain that Theo's mind and heart were equally involved. Even where Theo's letters are not preserved, the very ways in which Vincent expressed himself can be seen as contingent upon his brother's reactions. He consistently reported the details of his budget at length, and whenever he ran short of money he would set out in strategically persuasive fashion the reasons why it was desirable that Theo should send him more than usual, or dispatch his regular sum in advance of the customary date. Further, when discussing deeper concerns of his, he characteristically related his hopes and ambitions to the prospect of achieving sales through Theo's agency as a dealer, or to the possibility that his day-to-day living expenses might in some way be reduced.

Vincent expected from his brother both the reassurance that he was doing the right thing in continuing to paint and the faith that the money devoted to his support constituted a sound investment. The very tentativeness with which he phrased his continuous flood of inquiries and suggestions was motivated by the need to draw from this, his most permanent relationship with another human being, self-confidence both in his moral purpose and in his artistic future—so that he could order his doings accordingly and feel sustained by the knowledge that here at least the basic human needs of love and trust were under constant renewal. Because Theo on his part gave his mind to each new problem in turn, offered encouragement, invited clarifications and gave justifications for the best that he could do—because, in other words, his sympathy and solicitude were direct and immediate—the correspondence reflects a psychological relationship to which

the nearest parallel in normal experience would be the effect
upon a man and woman of years of living together. Far
from being a merely one-sided form of emotional release
the correspondence took on the function, chiefly under
Vincent's impetus, of intensifying a close blood-relationship
and common interest in the arts into a form in which two
people, spiritually and intellectually, depended on one another in an almost absolute way.

The written word and the painted image are of their
nature more deliberate than ordinary speech or action; and
the pattern of the letters, side by side with his art, gave
Vincent a necessary conviction that a shape and scheme
existed in a life which otherwise appeared troubled and lack-
ing in design. It was a shape and scheme which, by its very
continuity, implied the possibility of resistance to those forces
of psychic disturbance that might otherwise carry the brothers
apart and leave Vincent utterly alone—a palpable expression,
in fact, of a kinship that prolonged scrutiny of each other's
words and actions at close quarters would certainly have destroyed, to judge from the rank disharmony that sprang up
during the two-year period when they were living together.
When, at last, the same psychic disruptions took their toll on
one side, driving the painter to shoot himself, the results on
the other side were equally disastrous. Less than three months
after Vincent's funeral, Theo himself went mad while strain-
ing to organize a commemorative exhibition; he had to be
removed from the Paris scene and died immediately afterwards. There, in postscript form, lies the most dramatic of all
evidence as to what exactly the dependance between the two
brothers entailed.

The relationship by letter with his brother involved van
Gogh, as described, in the retailing of every kind of information that was of practical consequence : the state of his health
and energies and his consequent rate of work, the amount he
was spending on food and rent, the quality of the paints and
canvas that could be afforded on his behalf, the current
weather conditions and the supply of local people willing to
act as models, the disposal of his finished work and the choice

of suitable frames. Again and again the first things that he
had to report ran along lines like these :

As soon as I received your letter I bought 7 guilders'
worth of colour at once, so as to have some provisions
and to replenish my box. Throughout the week we have
had a lot of wind, storm and rain, and I went several
times to Scheveningen to see it. I brought home from
there two small seascapes . . . But another souvenir is
that I caught cold again, with all the outcomes you know,
and this forces me to stay at home for a few days . . .
When you next send money I shall buy some good
marten brushes, which are the real *drawing* brushes, as
I have discovered, for *drawing* a hand or a profile in
colour . . . My painting paper is also almost used up—
towards the first of September I shall have to buy a few
more supplies, but I shall not need more than the usual
allowance.

(August, 1882)

Thank you for your letter, but I've had a poor time of it
these last days; my money ran out on *Thursday,* and
so it proved a *hellishly long time* between then and
Monday noon. During these four days I have lived
mainly off coffee, 23 cups of it, with bread which I still
have to pay for. You are not to blame, if anyone is it's
me. Because I had a furious desire to see my pictures in
frames, and I had ordered rather too many of them for
my budget, seeing that the month's rent and the char-
woman had to be paid also. Even now, too, I shall be
drained dry to-day, since I must buy canvas also and prepare it myself . . . I am so much involved in work that
I cannot stop myself short. Rest assured, the bad weather
will stop me only too soon—the way it was today, yesterday and the day before as well.

(October, 1888)

And then too, alongside such prosaic details of an average

week's existence, the correspondence involved van Gogh in the formulation of a theory of art; that is, in statements setting out the nature and direction of his current artistic efforts and the conceptual significance for him of his completed pictures, or in discussions of the artists of the past that he admired most and the future of art as a whole. For example :

> I told you about my plan for a large drawing—well, I started it the very same day that I wrote to you . . . I have worked on it since then . . . I saw it clearly before me and wanted to carry it through. I made the composition simpler still, only one row of diggers. I sketched seven figures in it, five men and two women; the rest are smaller, on the second plane. It is the strongest drawing I have ever made. As to the conception . . . I adopted the manner of certain English artists, without thinking of imitating them—rather, no doubt, because I am attracted by the same kinds of thing in nature; these are taken up by relatively few, so that if one wants to make use of them one must seek a way to express what one feels and venture a little outside the ordinary rules in order to render them exactly as one wants.
>
> (June, 1883)

> Who will be in figure painting what Claude Monet is in landscape? . . . the painter of the future will be *a colourist such as has never yet been* . . . This painter who is to come—I can't imagine him living in little cafés, working away with several false teeth and going to the Zouaves' brothels, as I do. But I think that I am right when I feel that in a later generation it will come, and that as for us we must work as we can towards that end, without doubting and without wavering.
>
> (May, 1888)

Between practical information and pronouncements in the realm of art-theory, two aspects of Vincent's personality and vision revealed themselves as dominant. One of these was his conception of success, and the forms of self-criticism that attended it; the other was his propensity to relate every form of experience to his personal feelings, and instinctively find an identity for it in terms of this kind. For example:

> I think that it would greatly help me in my work if I had an opportunity to see more of printing, for instance . . . if I could get work in a printer's office or some such job, it would be a help rather than a hindrance . . . I am willing to try my hand at *anything* of that kind, especially if a living may be earned in that way. Indeed, I believe that there will come a time when it will not be necessary for me to earn a living in any other way than by painting.
>
> (November, 1883)

> I wanted to express how those ruins show that *for ages* the peasants have been laid to rest in the very fields which they dug up when alive—I wanted to say what a simple thing death and burial is, just as simple as the falling of an autumn leaf—just a bit of earth dug up—a wooden cross.
>
> (June, 1885)

In fact self-improvement, where his art was concerned, was for van Gogh both a moral and a technical affair. His work, as he saw it, could constantly be bettered by dint of attentive study and practice; to engage in this task in the right spirit and faith would at the same time bring a progressive deepening of his capacities for human understanding. What could be learnt on the technical side from past masters like Rembrandt and Delacroix and from the renewal of self-discipline from work to work merged with what was offered in the theoretical writings of men like Carlyle and Tolstoy, thinkers who believed that art could once more become supremely relevant to the workings of society as a whole. In his invariable optimism about the future, van Gogh set enormous store by the prospect of his making good—not so much because success would vindicate his presumed abilities, as because it would bear witness when it came to the essential "rightness" of the universe. It was not that the world owed him a debt and would eventually be compelled to pay it, but rather that the world would one day receive what he had it in him to give; and then success would bring repayment to those who had trusted in him, most especially his brother, and would increase the expectation at large for the generation of artists to which he belonged himself, and for other generations to come.

In the same way van Gogh's absolutely personal way of translating experience into words or paint merged the concrete and the theoretical as if there was no kind of a gap between them. The coalescence that he made between the visible aspects of experience and their internal or philosophic meaning was supremely intense; so intense, indeed, that it can almost be compared as a pattern of thought with the idea of the primitive tribesman that his wooden rain-god *is* the rain itself. Among many allusions in the letters illustrative of this point, the most recurrent are van Gogh's admiration of the works of earlier artists for the reflection he found in them of his own feelings for the subjects they had depicted, and, conversely, his use of some familiar pictorial image as a term of reference for identifying emotions aroused in him by particular sights and scenes:

Israëls' *An Old Man* . . . is sitting in a corner near the hearth, on which a small piece of peat is faintly glowing in the twilight. For it is a dark little cottage where that old man sits, an old cottage with a small white-curtained window. His dog, that has grown old with him, sits beside his chair—those two old friends look at each other, they look into each other's eyes, the dog and the man. And meanwhile the old man takes his tobacco pouch from his pocket and lights his pipe in the twilight; that is all, the twilight, the silence, the loneliness of those two old friends, the man and the dog, the understanding between those two . . .

(March, 1882)

One evening recently at Montmajour I saw a red sunset, shooting its rays on to the trunks and foliage of pines that were rooted in a conglomeration of rocks, colouring the trunks and foliage a fiery orange, while other pines on planes further back in space were silhouetted in Prussian blue against a sky of tender blue-green, cerulean. So it gave the effect of that Claude Monet, it was superb.

(May, 1888)

Whenever in fact van Gogh linked two categories of experience in order to recreate the newer of them for his own and his reader's benefit, it was characteristic of him to urge their complete identity.

Many artists of the past century who have written about their own work have done so *post facto* and with some kind of public audience in mind (however indirectly); most often they have tended to make their case by abstracting from current literary and æsthetic speculation whatever suited their individual requirements. Van Gogh's theory of art, on the other hand, set out to prescribe, not to explain. Indeed, in view of the inclusiveness of its recommendations, it lays claim to interpretation as a comprehensive artistic ideology.

Certainly the way of thinking in question here had an essential solidity, however far and wide it ranged in the promotion of more or less remote possibilities. Van Gogh's thought was centred always around a nucleus of ideological belief, and he modified his principles of life and art in the light of new experiences only to the degree and in the direction permitted by these underlying convictions. This was true of his visual experiences before both art and nature; of his experiences of literature—he was an avid reader all his life, constantly ready to identify himself with the central character of each book in turn; of his reactions to æsthetic theories that he read about or heard discussed. He was not averse to provisional experiment, but in the long run he always fell back on to fundamentals; the content of the Bible, for example, was as much of a fundamental to him at the end of his life as it had been in his youth, even though specific reference to it came to play a much smaller part in his letters than it had in the years when religion had offered him a practical goal. There is, therefore, a good deal of repetition in his correspondence—even between letters widely separated in date. There is perhaps also less of an expansion of ideas between 1880 and 1890 than one might expect a man of such extraordinary sensitivity to reveal between the ages of twenty-seven and thirty-seven. It would be wrong, however, to assume on these counts that van Gogh was inflexible either as a human being or as a thinker. The fact is rather that, given the way of thinking that he instinctively made his own, his development was bound to follow a self-extending pattern; and what this self-extension reached out for was the finding that in fundamentals lay the true and permanent source of creative energy.

The solidity of van Gogh's thought has a further and broader aspect. In terms of the cultural predicament of his time, this took the form of a passion for wholeness to set against the fragmentation of artistic sensibility that had increasingly characterized the nineteenth century. In terms of his personal life, it expressed a determination to keep his mind from, literally, going under—because van Gogh knew in advance what mental breakdown meant, he had the will and the drive to prescribe preventative measures. As he saw it, men were the poorer in that art was no longer something one felt called to, in the way that he did, as a way of transmitting the basic common truths of love and faith and suffering. Instead, the subjects of art had split apart from one another and so had its technical means (landscape and figure, for example, colour and modelling). It was above all necessary that art absorb back into its bloodstream the universals of human existence. Vincent's thought, then, required the firmness of bulwarks built against an encroaching tide: the tide of decadence and disorder. It had to command the presence of values, now lost, in works of art and literature transmitted from the past, through which the guide-lines of a continuing tradition were taken to run; and it needed also a wholesome and godly soundness of its own. Other nineteenth century thinkers before van Gogh—notably the proponents of the Gothic Revival—had similarly pleaded for restoration of the values of an earlier age, so that art and society, religion and culture might be re-unified. Certain of these thinkers had carried the Romantic concept of freedom to its logical conclusion, abandoning the present altogether in an advocacy of the past which was tantamount to escapism. But for van Gogh the processes of resistance and re-creation were not inherently divisible.

So finally one comes to the total picture of van Gogh which the *Letters to Theo* proclaim. Precisely where the paintings themselves might most readily tend to mislead, with their dynamic energy and their arbitrariness of colouring, these writings of the artist offer a firm corrective. They show an extraordinarily articulate man—anything but naïve and crazy, as a popular form of myth tends even now to imply. Van Gogh was in fact deeply interested in the contemporary intellectual scene and very much in control of his own destiny for all but a few weeks of his later career—the weeks in which he was actually struck down by his mental disease. Above all he was a man who committed himself to his work and his beliefs to the highest degree. " How difficult life must be," he wrote to Theo in one of his earliest letters, " if it is not strengthened and comforted by faith." And just a few weeks before his death he was able to say : " I still love art and life very much indeed."

M. R.

Cambridge, Mass.
August, 1962

MEMOIR OF VINCENT VAN GOGH

BY HIS SISTER-IN-LAW

The family name, van Gogh, is probably derived from the small town Gogh on the German frontier, but in the 16th century the van Goghs were already established in Holland. According to the "Annales Généalogiques" of Arnold Buchelius, there lived at that time a Jacob van Gogh at Utrecht "In the Owl behind the Town Hall," and Jan Jacob's son, who lived "In the Bible under the flax market," selling wine and books, was Captain of the Civil Guard.

Their coat-of-arms was a bar with three roses, which is still the family crest of the van Goghs.

In the 17th century we find many van Goghs occupying high offices of state in Holland. Johannes van Gogh, magistrate of Zutphen, is appointed High Treasurer of the Union in 1628; Michel van Gogh, at first Consul General in Brazil, afterwards treasurer of Zeeland, belongs to the Embassy that welcomes Charles II of England on his ascent to the throne in 1660. In about the same period, Cornelius van Gogh is a Remonstrant clergyman at Boskoop, and his son Matthias, at first a physician at Gouda, is afterwards clergyman at Moordrecht.

In the beginning of the 18th century the social standing of the family is somewhat lowered. A David van Gogh, who settled at The Hague, is a gold-wire drawer, like his eldest son Jan, who married Maria Stalvius, both belonging to the Walloon Church.

David's second son, Vincent (1729-1802), was a sculptor by profession, and is said to have been in Paris in his youth; in 1749 he was one of the Cent Suisses. With him the practice of art seems to have come into the family, together with fortune; he died single and left some money to his nephew Johannes (1763-1840), the son of his elder brother Jan van Gogh.

This Johannes was at first a gold-wire drawer like his father, but he afterwards became a Bible teacher, and clerk in the Cloister Church at The Hague. He was married to Johanna van der Vin of Malines, and their son Vincent (1789-1874) was enabled, by the legacy of his great uncle Vincent, to study theology at the University of Leiden. This Vincent, the grandfather of our painter, was a man of great intellect and extraordinarily strong sense of duty. At the Latin school he distinguished himself and won all prizes and testimonials; "the diligent and studious youth, Vincent van Gogh, fully deserves to be set up as an example to his fellow students for his good behaviour as well as for his persistent zeal," declares the rector of the school, Mr. de Booy, in 1805. At the University of Leiden he finishes his studies successfully, and graduates in 1811 at the age of twenty-two. He makes friends; his "album amicorum" preserves their memory in many Latin and Greek verses; a little silk embroidered wreath of violets and forget-me-nots, signed, E. H. Vrydag 1810, is wrought by the hand of the girl who became his wife as soon as he got the living of Benschop. They lived long and happily together, first at the parsonage of Benschop, then at Ochten, and from 1822 at Breda, where his wife died in 1857, and where he remained until his death, a deeply respected and honoured man.

Twelve children were born to them, of which one died in infancy; there was a warm cordial family feeling between them, and however far the children might drift apart in the world, they remained deeply attached and took part in each other's weal and woe. Two of the daughters married high placed officers, the Generals Pompe and 's Graeuwen; three remained single.

The six sons all occupied honourable positions in the world. Johannes went to sea and reached the highest rank in the navy, that of Vice-Admiral; at the time that he was commandant of the Navy Yard at Amsterdam in 1877, his nephew Vincent lived at his house for a time. Three sons became art dealers; the eldest Hendrik Vincent, "Uncle Hein" as he was called in the letters, had his business at first at Rotterdam

and afterwards settled at Brussels. Cornelius Marinus became
the head of the firm C. M. van Gogh, so well known in
Amsterdam. (His nephews often called him by his initials
C. M.). The third, who had the greatest influence on the
lives of his nephews Vincent and Theo, was Vincent, whose
health in his youth had been too weak to enable him to go to
college, to the deep regret of his father, who based the greatest expectations on him. He opened a little shop at The
Hague, where he sold colours and drawing materials, and
which he enlarged in a few years to an art gallery of
European renown. He was an extraordinarily gifted, witty,
and intelligent man, who had great influence in the world of
art at that time; Goupil in Paris offered him the partnership
in his firm, which only after van Gogh joined it reached its
highest renown. He settled in Paris and Mr. Tersteeg became the head of the firm in The Hague in his place. It
was here that Vincent and Theo got their first training in
business; Goupil was "the house" that played such a large
part in their lives, where Theo remained and made a success-
ful career, where Vincent worked for six years, and to which
his heart clung in spite of all, because in his youth it had
been to him "the best, the grandest, the most beautiful in
the world" (letter 332).

Only one of parson van Gogh's six sons chose the profession of his father. Theodorus (8 Febr. 1822-26 March 1885)
studied theology at Utrecht, graduated, and in 1849 got the
living of Groot-Zundert, a little village in Brabant on the
Belgian frontier, where he was confirmed by his father.
Theodorus van Gogh was a man of prepossessing appearance
("the handsome dominie" he was called by some), of a
loving nature and fine spiritual qualities, but he was not a
gifted preacher, and for twenty years he lived forgotten in
the small village of Zundert ere he was called to other
places, and even then only to small villages like Etten, Helvoirt and Nuenen. But in his small circle he was warmly
loved and respected, and his children idolized him.

In May 1851 he married Anna Cornelia Carbentus, who
was born in 1819 at The Hague, where her father Willem

Carbentus was a flourishing bookbinder. He had bound the first Constitution of Holland and thereby earned the title of "bookbinder to the King." His youngest daughter Cornelia was already married to Vincent van Gogh, the art dealer; his eldest daughter was the wife of the well-known clergyman Stricker at Amsterdam. The marriage of Theodorus van Gogh and Anna Carbentus was a very happy one. He found in his wife a helpmate, who shared with all her heart in his work; notwithstanding her own large family that gave her so much work, she visited his parishioners with him, and her cheerful and lively spirit was never quenched by the monotony of the quiet village life. She was a remarkable, lovable woman, who in her old age (she reached her 87th year), when she had lost her husband and three grown-up sons, still retained her energy and spirit and bore her sorrow with rare courage.

One of her qualities, next to her deep love of nature, was the great facility with which she could express her thoughts on paper; her busy hands, that were always working for others, grasped so eagerly not only needle and knitting needle, but also the pen. " I just send you a little word " was one of her favourite expressions, and how many of these " little words " came always just in time to bring comfort and strength to those to whom they were addressed. For almost twenty years they have been to myself a never failing source of hope and courage, and in this book, that is a monument to her sons, a word of grateful remembrance is due to their mother.

On the 30th of March 1852 a dead son was born at the vicarage of Zundert, but a year after on the same date Anna van Gogh gave birth to a healthy boy who was called Vincent Willem after his two grandfathers, and who in qualities and character, as well as in appearance took after his mother more than after his father. The energy and unbroken strength of will which Vincent showed in his life were, in principle, traits of his mother's character; from her also he took the sharp inquisitive glance of the eye from under the protruding eyebrows. The blonde complexion of both the parents turned in Vincent to a reddish hue; he was of medium height, rather broad shouldered, and his appearance made a strong, sturdy impression. This is also confirmed by the words of his mother, that none of the children *except* Vincent was very strong. A weaker constitution than his would certainly have broken down much sooner under the heavy strain Vincent put upon it. As a child he was of difficult temper, often troublesome and self-willed, and his bringing up was not fitted to counter-balance these faults, as the parents were very tender-hearted especially for their eldest. Once grandmother van Gogh, who had come from Breda to visit her children at Zundert, witnessed one of the naughty fits of little Vincent; she who had been taught by experience with her own twelve babies, took the little culprit by the arm and with a sound box on the ears put him out of the room. The tender-hearted mother was so indignant at this that she did not speak to her mother-in-law for a whole day, and only the sweet-tempered character of the young father succeeded in bringing about a reconciliation. In the evening he had a little carriage brought around, and drove the two women to the heath, where under the influence of a beautiful sunset they forgave each other.

Little Vincent had a great love for animals and flowers, and made all kinds of collections; of any extraordinary gift for drawing there was as yet no sign; it is only noted that at the age of eight he once modelled a little elephant of clay, that drew his parents' attention, but he destroyed it at once when according to his notion such a fuss was made about it. The same fate befell a very curious drawing of a cat, which his mother always remembered. For a short time he attended the village school, but his parents found that the intercourse with the peasant boys made him too rough, so a governess was sought for the children of the vicarage, whose number had meanwhile increased to six. Two years after Vincent a little daughter had been born and again two years later on the 1st of May 1857, came a son who was called after his father. After him came two sisters and a little brother. (The younger sister Willemien, who always lived with her mother, was the only one to whom Vincent wrote on rare occasions.) Theo was more tender and kind than his brother, who was four years older; he was more delicately built and finer featured, but of the same reddish fair complexion and he had the same light blue eyes, that sometimes darkened to a greenish blue.

In letter 338 Vincent himself describes the similarity and the difference in their looks, and in 1889 Theo wrote to me the following about Vincent's appearance, referring to Rodin's marble sculpture, the head of John the Baptist. " The sculptor has conceived an image of the precursor of Christ that exactly resembles Vincent. Yet he never saw him. That expression of sorrow, that forehead distorted by deep furrows, which denotes high thinking and iron self discipline, is Vincent's, though his is somewhat more sloping; the form of nose and structure of the head are the same." When I afterwards saw the marble I found in it a perfect resemblance to Theo.

The two brothers were strongly attached to each other from childhood; whereas the eldest sister, recalling youthful memories, speaks of Vincent's teasing ways, Theo only remembers that Vincent could invent such delightful games that once they made him a present of the most beautiful rose bush in their garden, to show their gratitude. Their childhood was full of the poetry of Brabant country life; they grew up among the cornfields, the heath and the pine forests, in that peculiar sphere of a village parsonage, the charms of which remained with them all their lives. It was not perhaps the best training to fit them for the hard struggle that awaited them both; they were still so very young, when they had to go out into the world, and with what bitter melancholy, and with what inexpressible home-sickness did they long during many years for the sweet home in the little village on the heath.

Vincent came back there several times, and remained always in appearance the " country boor," but Theo, who had become quite a refined Parisian, also kept in his heart something of the " Brabant boy " as he laughingly liked to call himself.

Like Vincent once rightly observes : " there will always remain in us something of the Brabant fields and heath," and when their father had died and mother had to leave the parsonage, he complains, "now there is none of us left in Brabant." When afterwards, in the hospital of Arles, the faithful brother visited him and in tender pity laid his head on the pillow beside him, Vincent whispered: "just like Zundert," and shortly after he writes: "during my illness I have seen every room in the house at Zundert, every path, every plant in the garden, the fields around, the neighbours, the churchyard, the church, our kitchen garden behind it— and even the magpie's nest in the high acacia in the church-yard" (letter 573).

So ineffaceable were those first sunny childhood's recollections. When Vincent was twelve years old he was sent to the boarding school of Mr. Provily at Zevenbergen; about this period not a single particular has been found, except that one of the sisters afterwards writes to Theo: "Do you remember how on mother's birthday Vincent used to come from Zevenbergen and what fun we had then?" Of friends in that time nothing is known.

When he was sixteen years old the choice of a profession became urgent and in this Uncle Vincent was consulted.

The latter, who meanwhile had acquired a large fortune as an art dealer, had been obliged by his feeble health to retire early from the strenuous business life in Paris—though still financially connected with the firm—and had settled at Princenhage, near his old father at Breda, and near his favourite brother at Zundert. Generally he passed the winter with his wife at Mentone in the south of France, and on his journey thither he always stayed some time at Paris, so that he remained in touch with the business. His beautiful country house at Princenhage had been enlarged by a gallery for his rare picture collection, and it was here that Vincent and Theo received their first impressions of the world of art. There was a warm cordial intercourse between the Zundert parsonage and the childless home of Princenhage; "the carriage" from there was always loudly cheered by the children at Zundert, for it brought many surprises of flowers, rare fruits and delicacies, while on the other hand the bright,

lively presence of the brother and sister from Zundert often
cast a cheerful sunbeam on the life of the patient at Princenhage. These brothers, Vincent and Theo too, who differed
but one year in age, were thoroughly attached to each other,
and the fact of their wives being sisters made the attachment
stronger still. What was more natural than that the rich art
dealer destined the young nephew who bore his name as his
successor in the firm—perhaps even to become his heir?

Thus in 1869 Vincent entered the house of Goupil & Co.,
at The Hague, as youngest employee under the direction of
Mr. Tersteeg, now a bright future seemed to lie in store for
him. He boarded with the family Roos on the Beestenmarkt,
where Theo afterwards lived also. It was a comfortable home
where his material needs were perfectly provided for, but
without any intellectual intercourse. This he found at the
homes of various relations and friends of his mother, where
he often visited, i.e. the Haanebeek's, the van Stockum's and
aunt Sophy Carbentus with her three daughters, one of whom
married our famous Dutch painter, A. Mauve, a second the
less known painter, A. le Comte. Tersteeg sent to the parents
good reports about Vincent's zeal and capacities, and like his
grandfather in his time, he is "the diligent studious youth"
whom everybody likes.

When he had been at The Hague for three years, Theo, who
is still at school at Oisterwijk (near Helvoirt, to which village
their father has been called), comes to stay with him for a
few days. It is after that visit in August 1872 that the correspondence between the two brothers begins, and from this,
now faded, yellow, almost childish, little note it is carried on
uninterruptedly until Vincent's death, when a half-finished
letter to Theo was found on him, of which the desponding
"que veux-tu" (what can I say) at the end, seems like a
gesture of resignation with which he parted from life.

The principal events of both their lives are mentioned in
the letters and are completed in this biographical notice by
particulars, either heard from Theo himself, or found in the
correspondence of the parents with Theo, also preserved in
full. (Vincent's letters to his parents were unfortunately de-

stroyed.) They date from January 1873, when Theo, then
only fifteen years old, went to Brussels to be also brought up
as an art dealer.

These letters, full of the tenderest love and care for the
boy who left home at such a tender age—" well Theo you are
quite a man now at fifteen," says his mother in one of her
letters; the boy to whom they clung so fondly, because he,
more than any of the other children, repays their love with
never failing tenderness and devotion, and grows up to be
" the crowning glory of their old age," as they were so fond
of calling him—these letters tell of all the small events of
daily life at the parsonage; what flowers were growing in the
garden, and how the fruit trees bore, if the nightingale had
been heard yet, what visitors had come, what the little sisters
and brother were doing, what was the text of father's sermon,
and among all this, many particulars about Vincent.

In 1873 the latter has been appointed to the firm in
London. When leaving The Hague he gets a splendid testi-
monial from Mr. Tersteeg, who also writes to the parents
that at the gallery everybody likes to deal with Vincent—
amateurs, clients, as well as painters—and that he certainly
will succeed in his profession. " It is a great satisfaction
that he can close the first period of his career in that way, and
withal he has remained just as simple as he was before,"
writes mother. At first everything goes well with him in
London; Uncle Vincent has given him introductions to some
of his friends and he busies himself with great pleasure in
his work; he earns a salary of £90 a year, and though living
is expensive, he manages to lay by some money to send
home now and then. Like a real business man he buys himself a top hat, " you cannot be in London without one," and
he enjoys his daily trips from the suburbs to the gallery in
Southampton Street in the city.

His first boarding-house is kept by two ladies, who own
two parrots, the place is good but somewhat expensive for
him, therefore he moves in August to the house of Mrs.
Loyer, a curate's widow from the south of France, who with
her daughter Ursula keeps a day school for little children.

Here he spends the happiest year of his life. Ursula makes a
deep impression upon him—" I never saw nor dreamt of anything like the love between her and her mother" he writes
to one of his sisters, and : " love her for my sake."

He does not mention it to his parents, for he has not even
confessed his love to Ursula herself,—but his letters home
are radiant with happiness. He writes that he enjoys his life
so much—" Oh fulness of rich life, your gift, Oh God."[1]

In September an acquaintance is going over to London
and undertook to carry a parcel for Vincent, and it is characteristic to hear that it contains, among other things, a bunch
of grass leaves and a wreath of oak leaves, made at home
during the holidays by Theo, who has meanwhile been appointed from Brussels to the House Goupil at The Hague.
Vincent must have something in his room to remind him of
the beloved fields and woods.

He celebrates a happy Christmas with the Loyers, and in
those days he sends home now and then a little drawing, from
his house and the street and from the interior of his room,
" so that we can exactly imagine how it looks, it is so well
drawn," writes his mother. In this period he seems to have
weighed the possibility of becoming a painter; afterwards
from Drenthe he writes to Theo : " how often have I stood
drawing on the Thames Embankment, as I went home from
Southampton Street in the evening—and the result was
nihil; had there been somebody then to tell me what perspective was, how much trouble would have been spared me, how
much farther should I be now."

At that time he now and then met Matthew Maris,[2] but was
too bashful to speak out freely to him, and shut up all his
longings and desires within himself—he had still a long road
of sorrow to go ere he could reach his goal.

In January his salary is raised and until spring his letters
remain cheerful and happy; he intends to visit Holland in
July and before that time seems to have spoken to Ursula of
his love. Alas it turns out that she is already engaged to

[1] First line of a well known Dutch poem.
[2] Famous Dutch painter, living in London.

somebody, who boarded with them before Vincent came. He tries all his influence to make her break this engagement but does not succeed, and with this first great sorrow there comes a change in his character; when he comes home for the holidays he is thin, silent, dejected, a changed being. But he *draws* a great deal. Mother writes: " Vincent made many a nice drawing, he drew the bedroom window and the front door, all that part of the house, and also a large sketch of those houses in London upon which their window looks out; it is a delightful talent, that can be of great value to him."

Accompanied by his eldest sister, who wants to find a situation, he returns to London; he takes furnished rooms in Ivy Cottage, 395 Kensington New Road, and there without any family life he grows more and more silent and depressed and also more and more religious.

His parents were glad he left the Loyers—" there were too many secrets and it was not a family like others; but it must have been a great disappointment to him that his illusions were not realized," father writes, and mother complains, " the evenings are so long already and his work finishes early, he must be lonely, if it only does not harm him."

They feel uneasy and worried about his solitary, secluded life. Uncle Vincent also insists upon his mixing more with other people, " that is just as necessary as to learn business "; but the depressed mood continues, letters home grow more and more scarce, and mother begins to think that the London fog depresses him and that even a temporary change might do him good—" poor boy, he means so well, but I believe things are very hard for him just now."

In October 1874, Uncle Vincent effects indeed a short removal to the firm in Paris, but Vincent himself is little pleased by this, in fact he is so angry that he does not write home, to the great grief of his parents. " He is only in a bad temper," his sister says, and Theo comforts, " he is doing all right."

Towards the end of December he returns to London where he takes the same rooms and leads the same retired life. Now for the first time the word *eccentric* is applied to him. His love for drawing has ceased, but he reads much and the quotation from Renan that closes the London period clearly shows what filled his thoughts and how he aimed even then at the high ideal: "to sacrifice all personal desires, to realize great things, to obtain nobleness of mind, to surpass the vulgarity in which the existence of nearly all individuals is spent." He did not know yet which way he had to go to reach that aim.

In May 1875, he is placed permanently in Paris and assigned especially to the picture gallery, where he feels himself quite out of place; he is more at home in his "cabin," the little room at Montmartre where, morning and evening, he reads the Bible with his young friend, Harry Gladwell, than among the mondaine Parisian public.

His parents read from his letters that things are not going well, and when he comes home at Christmas and everything is talked over, father writes to Theo: "I almost think that Vincent had better leave Goupil in two or three months; there is so much that is good in him, but yet it may be necessary for him to change his position, he is certainly not happy." And they love him too well to persuade him to stay in a place where he would be unhappy; he wants to live for others, to be useful, to bring about something great, *how* he does not know as yet, but *not* in an art gallery. On his return from Holland he has the decisive interview with Mr. Boussod (the son-in-law and successor of Mr. Goupil) that ends with his dismissal on the 1st of April, and he accepts it without bringing in any excuses for himself. One of the grievances against him was that he had gone home to Holland for Christmas and New Year, the busiest time for business in Paris.

In his letters he seems to take it rather lightly, but he feels how gloomily and threateningly the clouds begin to gather around him. At the age of twenty-three years he is now thrown out of employment, without any chance of a better career; Uncle Vincent is deeply disappointed in his namesake and washes his hands of him; his parents are well-meaning, but they cannot do much for him having been obliged to touch their capital for the education of their children. (The pastor's salary was about 820 guilders a year.) Vincent has had his share, now others must have theirs. It seems that Theo who becomes so soon the helper and adviser of all, has already at that time suggested Vincent's becoming a painter, but for the moment he will not hear of it. His father speaks of a position in a museum and advises him to open a small art gallery for himself, as Uncle Vincent and Uncle Cor have done before; he would then be able to follow his own ideas about art and be no longer obliged to sell pictures which he considered bad—but his heart again draws him to England and he plans to become a teacher.

Through an advertisement, in April 1876 he gets a position in Ramsgate at Mr. Stokes', who moves his school in July to Isleworth. He received only board and lodging, but no salary, so he soon accepts another position at the somewhat richer school of Mr. Jones, a Methodist preacher, where Vincent acts finally as a kind of curate.

His letters home are gloomy. "It seems as if something were threatening me," he writes, and his parents perceive full well that teaching does not satisfy him. They suggest his studying for a French or German college certificate, but he will not hear of it. "I wish he could find some work in connection with art or nature," writes his mother, who understands what is going on within him. With the force of despair he clings to religion, in which he tries to find satisfaction for his craving for beauty, as well as for his longing to live for others. At times he seems to intoxicate himself with the sweet melodious words of the English texts and hymns, the romantic charm of the little village church, and the lovely, holy atmosphere that envelops the English service. His letters in those days bear an almost morbid sensitiveness. Often and often he speaks about a position related to the church—but when he comes home for Christmas, it is decided that he will not go back to Isleworth, because there is absolutely no prospect for the future. He remains on friendly terms with Mr. Jones, who afterwards comes to stay a few days at the Nuenen parsonage, and whom he later meets in

Belgium. Once more Uncle Vincent uses his influence and procures for him a place in the bookshop of Blussé and Braam at Dordrecht. He accepts it, but without great enthusiasm. Characteristic are the words written to Theo by one of the sisters. " You think that he is something more than an ordinary human being, but I think it would be much better if he thought himself just an ordinary being." Another sister writes, " His religion makes him absolutely dull and unsociable."

To preach the Gospel still seems to him the only desirable thing, and at last an attempt is made to enable him to begin the study of Theology. The uncles in Amsterdam promised to give their aid; he can live with Uncle Jan van Gogh, Commandant of the Navy Yard, which will be a great saving of expenses : Uncle Stricker finds out the best teacher in the classical languages, the well-known Dr. Mendes da Costa, and gives him some lessons himself; in the art gallery at Uncle Cor's he can satisfy his love for pictures and prints and so everybody tries to make it easy for him, all except Uncle Vincent, who is strongly opposed to the plan and will not help to forward it—in which he proved to be right after all. Full of courage Vincent sets to work, he must first prepare himself for a State examination before he can be admitted to the University; it will take him seven years ere he is ready; anxiously the parents ask themselves whether he will have the strength to persevere, and whether he who has never been used to regular study will be able to force himself to it at the age of twenty-four.

That period in Amsterdam from May 1877 to 1878 is one long tale of woe. After the first half-year Vincent begins to lose ardour and courage; the writing of exercises and the study of grammar is not what he wants—he desires to comfort and cheer people by bringing them the Gospel,—and surely he does not need so much learning for that! He actually longs for *practical* work, and when at last his teacher also perceives that Vincent never will succeed, he advises him to give up the study. In the " Handelsblad " of the 30th of November 1910, Dr. Mendes da Costa writes his personal recollections of the afterwards so famous pupil, of whom he tells many characteristic particulars : his nervous, strange appearance, that yet was not without charm, his fervent intention to study well, his peculiar habit of self-discipline, self-chastisement, and finally his total unfitness for regular study. Not along that path was he to reach his goal! Openly he confesses that he is glad things have gone so far and that he can look towards his future with more courage than when he devoted himself hopelessly to Theological study, which period he afterwards called "the worst time of his life."

He will remain "humble" and now wants to become an Evangelist in Belgium; for this no certificates are required, no Latin nor Greek; only three months at the school of Evangelisation at Brussels—where lessons are free and only board and lodging are charged for—and he can get his nomination. In July he travels thither with his father, accompanied by Mr. Jones who on his way to Belgium has spent a few days with them at Etten, and together they visit the different members of the Committee of Evangelization : the Rev. van den Brink from Rousselaere, Rev. Pietersen from Malines, and Rev. de Jong from Brussels. Vincent explained his case clearly and made a very good impression. His father writes : " His stay abroad and that last year at Amsterdam have not been quite fruitless after all, and when he takes the trouble to exert himself he shows that he has learned and observed much in the school of life," and Vincent consequently is accepted as a pupil. But the parents regard this new experiment with fresh anxiety : " I am always so afraid that wherever Vincent may be or whatever he may do, he will spoil everything by his eccentricity, his queer ideas and views on life," his mother writes, and his father adds, " It grieves us so when we see that he literally knows no joy of life, but always walks with bent head, whilst we did all in our power to bring him to an honourable position! It seems as if he deliberately chooses the most difficult path."

In fact that was Vincent's aim—to humble himself, to forget himself, to sacrifice himself, " mourir à soi-même," (to sacrifice every personal desire), that was the ideal he tried to reach as long as he sought his refuge in religion, and he never did a thing by halves. But to follow the paths trodden by others, to submit to the will of other people, that was not in his character, he wanted to work out his own salvation. Towards the end of August he arrives at the school at Brussels, which had only been recently opened and counted but three pupils; in the class of Mr. Bokma he certainly was the most advanced, but he does not feel at home at the school, he is "like a fish out of water" he says, and is ridiculed for his peculiarities in dress and manners. He also misses the talent of extemporizing and is therefore obliged to read his lectures from manuscript; but the greatest objection against him is, "he is not submissive," and when the three months have elapsed he does not get his nomination. Though he writes it (in letter 126) in an off-hand way to Theo, he seems to have been greatly upset by it. His father receives a letter from Brussels, probably from the school, saying that Vincent is weak and thin, does not sleep, and is in a nervous and excited state, so that the best thing will be to come and take him home.

Immediately he travels to Brussels and succeeds in arranging everything for the best. Vincent goes at his own risk to the Borinage where he boards at 30 fr. a month with M. Van der Haegen, Rue de L'Eglise 39, at Paturages near Mons. He teaches the children in the evening, visits the poor and gives lectures from the Bible, and when in January the Committee meets, he will again try to get a nomination. The intercourse with the people there pleases him very well; in his leisure hours he draws large maps of Palestine, of which his father orders four at 10 fr. apiece, and at last, in January 1879, he gets a temporary nomination for six months at Wasmes at 50 fr. a month for which he must give Bible lectures, teach the children and visit the sick—the work of his heart. His first letters from there are very contented and he devotes himself heart and soul to his work, especially the practical part of it; his greatest interest is in nursing the sick and wounded. Soon, however, he falls back to the old exaggerations—he tries to put into practice the doctrines of Jesus, gives away everything, his money, clothes and bed, he leaves the good board-ing-house at Denis, in Wasmes, and retires to a miserable hut where every comfort is wanting. Already they had written to his parents about it and when, towards the end of February, the Rev. Rochelieu comes for inspection, the bomb explodes, for so much zeal is too much for the committee and a person who neglects himself so cannot be an example to other people. The Church Council at Wasmes have a meeting and they agree that if he does not listen to reason he will lose his position. He himself takes it rather coolly. "What shall we do now?" he writes, "Jesus was also very calm in the storm, perhaps it must grow worse before it grows better." Again his father goes to him, and succeeds in stilling the storm; he brings him back to the old boarding-house, advises him to be less exaggerated in his work, and for some time everything is all right, at least he writes that no reproofs are made. About that time a heavy mine explosion occurs and a strike breaks out, so Vincent can devote himself completely to the miners, and his mother in her naïve religious faith writes, "Vincent's letters that contain so many interesting things prove that with all his singularities he yet shows a warm interest in the poor and that surely will not remain unobserved by God." In that same time he also writes that he tries to *sketch the dresses and tools of the miners and will show them when he comes home.* In July bad tidings come again, "he does not comply with the wishes of the committee and nothing will change him. It seems that he is deaf to all remarks that are made to him," writes his mother, and when the six months of his temporary nomination are past, he is not appointed again, but they give him three months to look out for another position. He leaves Wasmes and travels on foot to Brussels to ask the Rev. Pietersen, who has moved thither from Malines, for advice. The latter paints in his leisure hours and has a studio, which probably was the reason why Vincent went to him for help. Tired and hot, exhausted and in a nervous condition he arrives there and so neglected was his appear-ance that the daughter of the house who opened the door for him was frightened, called for her father and ran away. The

Rev. Pietersen received him kindly; procured him good lodgings for the night, invited him to his table the next day, showed him the studio, and as Vincent had brought some of his sketches of the miners, they probably talked as much about drawing and painting as about Evangelization.

"Vincent gives me the impression of somebody who stands in his own light," writes the Rev. Pietersen to his parents, and mother adds, "how lucky it is that still he always finds somebody who helps him on, as now the Rev. Pietersen has."

In accordance with the latter's advice, Vincent resolves to stay in the Borinage at his own expense, as he cannot be in the service of the committee, and that he will board with the Evangelist Frank, at Cuesmes. About the middle of August, at his parents' request, he visits them again at Etten. "He looks well, except for his clothes, he reads Dickens all day and speaks only when he is addressed, about his future not a single word," writes his mother. What could he say about his future? Did it ever look more hopeless than it did now? His illusion of bringing through the Gospel comfort and cheer into the miserable lives of the miners had gradually been lost in the bitter strife between doubt and religion, which he had to fight at that time, and which made him lose his former faith in God. (The Bible texts and religious reflections which became more and more rare in his last letters now stop entirely.) No other thing has taken its place yet; he draws much and reads much, among others, Dickens, Beecher Stowe, Victor Hugo, and Michelet, but it is all done without system or aim. Back in the Borinage he wanders about without work, without friends and very often without bread, for though he receives money from home and from Theo, they cannot give him more than is strictly necessary, and as it comes in at very irregular times and Vincent is a very poor financier, there are days and even weeks when he is quite without money.

In October Theo, who has got a permanent position at Goupil's in Paris, comes to visit him on his journey thither and tries in vain to bring him to some fixed plan for the future; he is not yet ripe to take any resolution; before he becomes conscious of his real power he has still to struggle through the awful winter of 1879-80, that saddest, most hopeless time of his never very fortunate life. In these days he undertakes, with ten francs in his pocket, the hopeless expedition to Courrières, the dwelling place of Jules Breton, whose pictures and poems he so much admires, and with whom he secretly hopes to come in contact in some way or other. But the only thing that becomes visible to him is the inhospitable exterior of Breton's newly built studio and he lacks the courage to introduce himself. Disappointed in his hope, he has to undertake the long journey home; his money is all spent, generally he sleeps in the open air or in a hay loft. Sometimes he exchanges a drawing for a piece of bread, and he undergoes so much fatigue and want that his health always suffered from the consequences. In spring he comes once more to the vicarage of Etten and speaks again about going to London. " If he really wants it, I shall enable him to go," writes his father, but finally he returns again to the Borinage and lives that summer of 1880 at the house of the miner Charles Decrucq at Cuesmes. There he writes in July the wonderfully touching letter (133) that tells of what is going on in his innermost self—" My only anxiety is what can I do . . . could I not be of use, and good for something?" It is the old wish, the old longing to serve and comfort humanity, which made him write afterwards, when he had found his calling, " And in a picture I wish to say something that would console me as music does." Now in the days of deepest discouragement and darkness at last the light begins to dawn. Not in books shall he find satisfaction, not in literature find his work, as his letters sometimes suggested; he turns back to his old love, " I said to myself, I'll take up my pencil again, I will take up drawing, and from that moment everything has changed for me." It sounds like a cry of deliverance, and once more, " do not fear for me, if I can continue my work I will succeed." At last he has found his work and herewith the mental equilibrium is restored; he no longer doubts of himself and however difficult or heavy his life may become the inward serenity, the conviction of his own calling never more deserts him.

The little room in the house of the miner Decrucq, which he has to share with the children, is his first studio. There he begins his painter's career with the first original drawing of miners who go to work in the early morning. There he copies with restless activity the large drawings after Millet, and when the room is getting too narrow for him, he takes his work out into the garden.

When the cold autumn weather prevents his doing this, and as his surroundings at Cuesmes are getting too narrow for him, he moves in October to Brussels where he settles in a small hotel on the Bd. du Midi 72. He is longing to see pictures again, but above all he hopes to become acquainted with other artists. Deep in his heart there was such a great longing for sympathy, for kindness and friendship, and though his difficult character generally prevented him from finding this and left him isolated in life, yet he always kept on longing for somebody with whom he could live and work.

Theo, who meanwhile had acquired a good position in Paris, could now assist him in word and deed. He brought Vincent into relation with the young Dutch painter van Rappard, who had worked some time in Paris and now studied at the academy at Brussels. At first the acquaintance did not progress, for the outward difference between the rich young nobleman and the neglected wanderer from the Borinage was too great to ripen the acquaintance at once into friendship; yet the artistic taste and opinions of both were too similar for them not to find each other; a friendship arose—perhaps the only one that Vincent ever had in Holland—it lasted for five years and then was broken through a misunderstanding, which van Rappard always regretted, though he acknowledged that intercourse with Vincent was very difficult.

" I remember as if it happened yesterday the moment of our first meeting at Brussels when he came into my room at nine o'clock in the morning, how at first we did not get on very well together, but so much the better after we had worked together a few times," writes van Rappard to Vincent's mother after the latter's death. And again, " whoever has witnessed this wrestling, struggling and sorrowful existence could not but feel sympathy for the man who demanded so much of himself, that it ruined body and mind. He belonged to the race that produces the great artists.

" Though Vincent and I had been separated the last years by a misunderstanding which I have often regretted—I have never ceased to remember him and the time we spent together with great sympathy.

" Whenever in the future I shall remember that time, and it is always a delight for me to recall the past, the characteristic figure of Vincent will appear to me in such a melancholy but clear light, the struggling and wrestling, fanatic, gloomy Vincent, who used to flare up so often and was so irritable, but who still deserved friendship and admiration for his noble mind and highly artistic qualities."

Vincent's own opinion of van Rappard is clearly shown in his letters. A second acquaintance that Vincent made through Theo, with the painter Roelofs, was of less-during importance. Roelofs' advice to enter the Academy was not followed by Vincent, perhaps they did not admit him because he was not far enough advanced, but probably he had more than enough of academical institutions and theories, and in painting as well as in theology he preferred to go his own way; that is the reason he did not come into contact with other Dutch painters who were at that same time at the Academy at Brussels, for instance, Haverman.

He studied anatomy by himself, drew diligently from the living model, and from a letter to his father it seems that he took lessons in perspective from a poor painter at 1.50 fr. a lesson of two hours : it has not been possible to fix the name of the painter, it may have been Madiol.

At the end of the winter when van Rappard goes away, in whose studio he has often worked because his own little bedroom was too small, he longs for other surroundings, especially for the country; the expenses in Brussels are also somewhat heavy, and he thinks it will be cheapest to go to his parents at Etten where he has board and lodging free and can use all money he receives for his work.

He stays there for eight months, and this summer of 1881 is again a happy time for him. First, van Rappard comes to stay with him and he too always remembers with pleasure his stay at the vicarage, " And my visit at Etten! I see you still sitting at the window when I came in," he writes to Vincent's mother in the letter quoted above, " I still enjoy that beautiful walk we all took together that first evening, through the fields and along the small path! And our excursions to Seppen, Passievaart, Liesbosch, I often look through my sketch books for them."

In the beginning of August Theo comes over from Paris; shortly after Vincent makes an excursion to The Hague to consult about his work with Mauve, who firmly encourages him, so that he continues with great animation, and finally in those days he meets for the second time a woman who has great influence on his life. Among the guests who spent that summer at the vicarage at Etten was a cousin from Amsterdam—a young widow with her little four-year-old son. Quite absorbed in her grief over the loss of her husband, whom she had loved so tenderly, she was unconscious of the impression which her beauty and touching sorrow made on the cousin, who was a few years her junior. " He was so kind to my little boy," she said when she afterwards remembered that time. Vincent who had great love for children, tried to win the heart of the mother by great devotion to the child. They walked and talked much together, and he has also drawn a portrait of her (which seems to have been lost), but the thought of a more intimate relation did not occur to her, and when Vincent spoke to her at last about his love, a very decided *no* was the immediate reply. She went back to Amsterdam and never saw him again. But Vincent could not abide by her decision, and with his innate tenacity he keeps on persevering and hoping for a change in her feelings for him; when his letters are not answered, he accuses both his and her parents of opposing the match, and only a visit to

Amsterdam, where she refuses to see him, convinces him of the utter hopelessness of his love.

" He fancied that he loved me," she said afterwards, but for him it was sad earnest, and her refusal becomes a turning point in his life. If she had returned his love it would perhaps have been a spur to him to acquire a social position, he would have had to provide for her and her child; as it is he loses all worldly ambition and in the future lives only for his work, without taking one step to make himself independent. He cannot bear to stay in Etten any longer, he has become irritable and nervous, his relations to his parents become strained, and after a violent altercation with his father, in December he leaves suddenly for The Hague.

The two years he spends there are, for his work, a very important period of which his letters give a perfect description. His low spirits rise at first, by the change of surroundings and the intercourse with Mauve, but the feeling of having been slighted and wronged does not leave him and he feels himself utterly abandoned. When he meets in January a poor neglected woman approaching her confinement, he takes her under his protection, partly from pity but also to fill the great void in his life. " I hope there is no harm in his so-called model. Bad connections often arise from a feeling of loneliness, of dissatisfaction," writes his father to Theo, who is always the confidant of both parties and has to listen to all the complaints and worries; father is not far wrong. Vincent could not be alone, he wanted to live for somebody, he wanted a wife and children, and as the woman he loved had rejected him, he took the first unhappy woman who crossed his path, with children that were not his own. At first he feigns to be happy and tries to convince Theo in every letter how wisely and well he has acted, and the touching care and tenderness with which he surrounds the woman when she leaves the hospital after her confinement, strike us painfully when we think on whom that treasure of love was lavished. He prides himself now on having a family of his own, but when their living together has become a fact and he is continually associated with a coarse, uneducated woman,

marked by smallpox, who speaks with a low accent and has
a spiteful character, who is addicted to liquor and smokes
cigars, whose past life has not been irreproachable, and who
draws him into all kinds of intrigues with her family,[1] he
soon writes no more about his home life; even the posing,
by which she won him (she sat for the beautiful drawing,
"Sorrow"), and of which he had expected so much, soon
ceases altogether. This unfortunate adventure deprives him
of the sympathy of all in The Hague who took an interest in
him. Neither Mauve nor Tersteeg could approve of his taking
upon himself the cares of a family, and such a family! while
he was financially dependent on his younger brother. Ac-
quaintances and relatives are shocked to see him walk about
with such a slovenly woman; nobody cares to associate with
him any longer and his home life is such that nobody comes
to visit him. The solitude around him becomes greater and
greater and as usual it is only Theo who understands and
continues to help him.

When the latter comes to visit Vincent for the second time
in The Hague, in the summer of 1883, and witnesses the situation—finds the household neglected, everything in bad condition and Vincent deeply in debt—he too advises to let the
woman go her own way as she is not fit for a regulated life.
She herself had already felt that things could not continue like
that, because Vincent wants too much money for his painting
to leave enough for the support of her and the children, and
she was already planning with her mother to earn money in
another way. Vincent himself feels that Theo is right, and
in his heart he longs for a change of surroundings, and liberty
to go where his work calls him, but it costs him a bitter
struggle to give up what he had taken upon himself, and to
leave the poor woman to her fate. Till the last he defends
her, and excuses her for her faults with the sublime words,
"she has never seen what is good, so how can she be good?"

In those days of inward strife he allows Theo to read
deeper than ever into his heart. These last letters from The

[1] This is in fact an exaggerated picture of the woman's character.
[Ed.]